BOOK 2

THE BEST OF

Martha Mier

A Special Collection of 7 Late Elementary to Early Intermediate Favorite Piano Solos

D1542359

Martha Mier's sheet music solos have become student favorites over the years. Her love of teaching, combined with her talent for composing, has produced many pieces that appeal to students of all ages.

This special collection includes some of Martha's personal favorite and best-selling sheet music solos. Each piece is a special treat. Turn the page and find out why everyone loves the music of Martha Mier.

Contents

Cover art: Franz Marc, German, 1880–1916, The Bewitched Mill, oil on canvas, 1913, 130.2 x 91.1 cm
Arthur Jerome Eddy Memorial Collection, 1931.522 ; photograph © 1995 The Art Institute of Chicago
Cover design: Ted Engelbart   Music engraving: Tom Gerou

Taco Rock

Read carefully

Martha Mier

Moderately

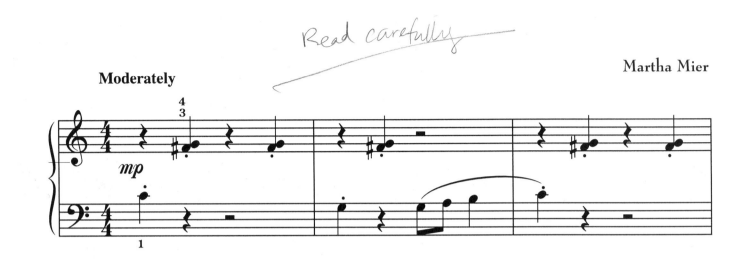

Thistles in the Wind

Martha Mier

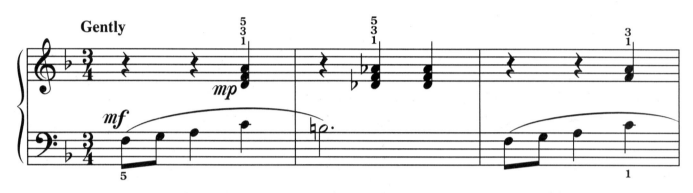

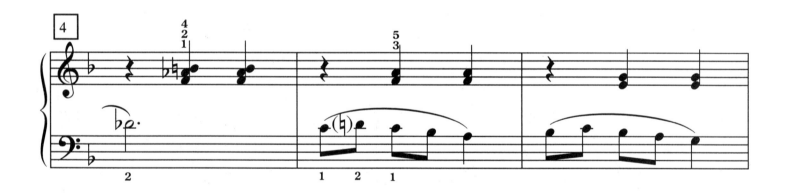

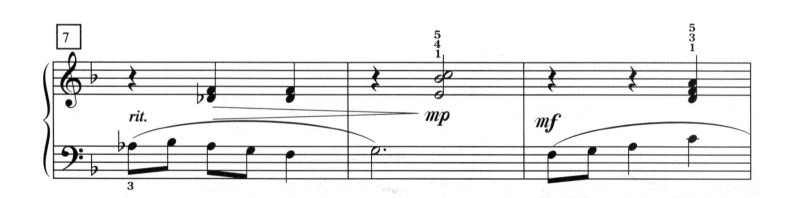

Green Dragonflies

Martha Mier

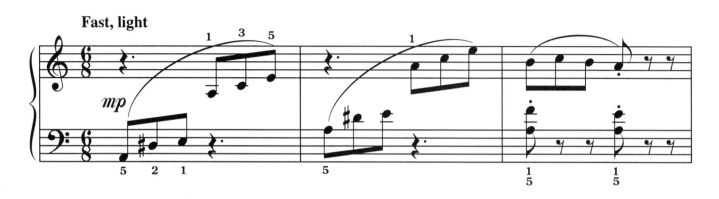

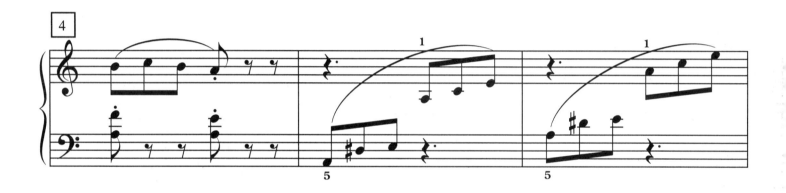

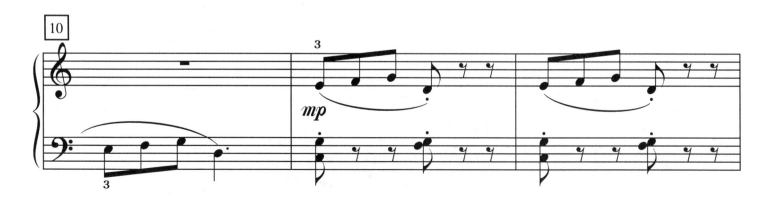

Appaloosa Pony

Martha Mier

Jack-O'-Lantern Jamboree

Martha Mier

for Marissa Brittany

Lady Brittany's Ballad

Martha Mier

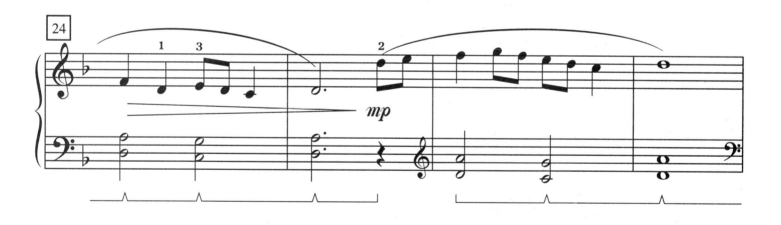

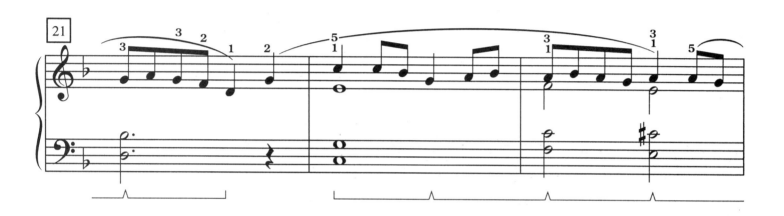

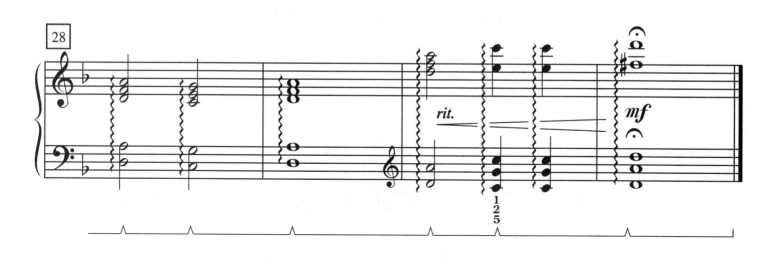

Petite Gavotte

Martha Mier

With dignity and grace

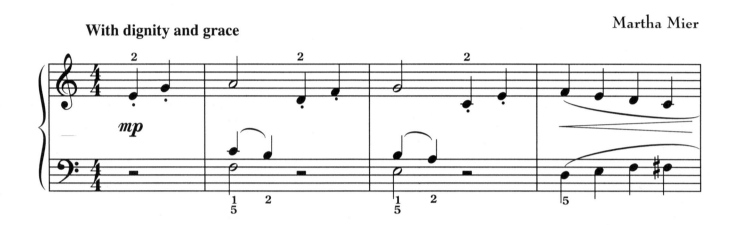

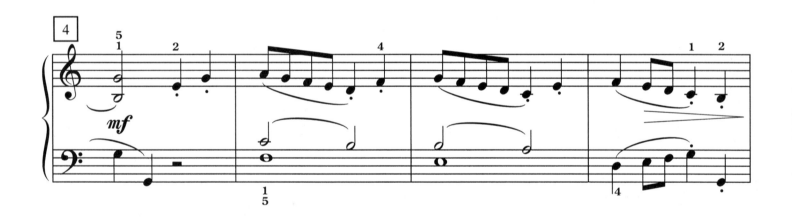

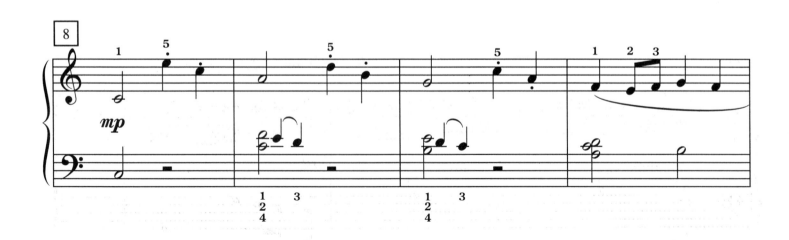